www.EffortlessMath.com

... So Much More Online!

✓ FREE Math lessons

✓ More Math learning books!

✓ Mathematics Worksheets

✓ Online Math Tutors

Need a PDF version of this book?

Visit www.EffortlessMath.com

5 SSAT Lower Level Math Practice Tests

Extra Practice to Help Achieve an

Excellent Score

By

Reza Nazari

ISBN: 978-1-64612-246-2

Published by: Effortless Math Education

www.EffortlessMath.com

Description

5 SSAT Lower Level Math Practice Tests, which reflects the 2020 and 2021 test guidelines, is a comprehensive practice book to help your students hone their math skills, overcome their exam anxiety, and boost their confidence -- and do their best to succeed on the SSAT Lower Level Math Test. Five complete and realistic SSAT Lower Level Math practice tests help students learn how the test is structured and what mathematics concepts they need to master before the test day. The practice test questions are followed by detailed answers and explanations to help test takers find their weak areas, learn from their mistakes, and raise their SSAT Lower Level Math score.

The surest way to succeed on SSAT Lower Level Math Test is with intensive practice in every math topic tested-- and that's what you will get in *5 SSAT Lower Level Math Practice Tests*. This SSAT Lower Level Math new edition has been updated to replicate questions appearing on the most recent SSAT Lower Level Math tests. This is a precious learning tool for SSAT Lower Level Math test takers who need extra practice in math to improve their SSAT Lower Level Math score. After taking the SSAT Lower Level Math practice tests in this book, students will have solid foundation and adequate practice that is necessary to succeed on the SSAT Lower Level Math test. **This book is your student's ticket to ace the SSAT Lower Level Math test!**

5 SSAT Lower Level Math Practice Tests includes many exciting and unique features to help your students improve their test scores, including:

- Content 100% aligned with the 2020 - 2021 SSAT test
- Prepared by SSAT Math instructors and test experts
- Complete coverage of all essential SSAT Lower Level Math concepts and topics which students will be tested
- Detailed answers and explanations for every SSAT Lower Level Math practice question to help students learn from their mistakes
- 5 complete practice tests (featuring new question types) with detailed answers
- And much more!

This SSAT Lower Level Math practice book and other Effortless Math Education books are used by thousands of students each year to help them review core content areas, brush-up in math, discover their strengths and weaknesses, and achieve their best scores on the SSAT Lower Level test.

About the Author

Reza Nazari is the author of more than 100 Math learning books including:

– Math and Critical Thinking Challenges: For the Middle and High School Student

– ACT Math in 30 Days.

– ASVAB Math Workbook 2018 – 2019

– Effortless Math Education Workbooks

– and many more Mathematics books ...

Reza is also an experienced Math instructor and a test–prep expert who has been tutoring students since 2008. Reza is the founder of Effortless Math Education, a tutoring company that has helped many students raise their standardized test scores—and attend the colleges of their dreams. Reza provides an individualized custom learning plan and the personalized attention that makes a difference in how students view math.

You can contact Reza via email at:

reza@EffortlessMath.com

Find Reza's professional profile at:

goo.gl/zoC9rJ

Contents

SSAT Lower Level Math Practice Tests

The SSAT, or Secondary School Admissions Test, is a standardized test to help determine admission to private elementary, middle and high schools.

There are currently three Levels of the SSAT:

- ✓ Lower Level (for students in 3rd and 4th grade)
- ✓ Middle Level (for students in 5th-7th grade)
- ✓ Upper Level (for students in 8th-11th grade)

There are four sections on the SSAT Lower Level Test:

- ✓ Quantitative (Mathematics) section: 30 questions, 30 minutes.
- ✓ Verbal section: 30 questions, 20 minutes.
- ✓ Reading section: 7 short passages, 28 questions, 30 minutes.
- ✓ Writing sample: 15 minutes to write a short passage

In this book, there are five complete SSAT Lower Level Quantitative practice tests. Take these tests to see what score you'll be able to receive on a real SSAT Lower Level test.

Good luck!

Time to refine your skill with a practice examination

Take a practice SSAT Lower Level Mathematics Test to simulate the test day experience. After you've finished, score your test using the answer key.

Before You Start

- You'll need a pencil and a timer to take the test.

- After you've finished the test, review the answer key to see where you went wrong.

- Use the answer sheet provided to record your answers. (You can cut it out or photocopy it)

- You will receive 1 point for every correct answer. You won't receive any point for wrong or skipped answers.

Calculators are NOT permitted for the SSAT Lower Level Test

Good Luck!

SSAT Lower Level Math

Practice Test 1

2020 - 2021

Total number of questions: 30

Total time for this test: 30 Minutes

Calculator is NOT permitted for SSAT Lower Level Math Test.

1

SSAT Lower Level Mathematics Practice Test Answer Sheet

Remove (or photocopy) this answer sheet and use it to complete the practice test.

SSAT Lower Level Mathematics Practice Test Answer Sheet

SSAT Lower Level Practice Test 1

1	Ⓐ Ⓑ Ⓒ Ⓓ Ⓔ	11	Ⓐ Ⓑ Ⓒ Ⓓ Ⓔ	21	Ⓐ Ⓑ Ⓒ Ⓓ Ⓔ
2	Ⓐ Ⓑ Ⓒ Ⓓ Ⓔ	12	Ⓐ Ⓑ Ⓒ Ⓓ Ⓔ	22	Ⓐ Ⓑ Ⓒ Ⓓ Ⓔ
3	Ⓐ Ⓑ Ⓒ Ⓓ Ⓔ	13	Ⓐ Ⓑ Ⓒ Ⓓ Ⓔ	23	Ⓐ Ⓑ Ⓒ Ⓓ Ⓔ
4	Ⓐ Ⓑ Ⓒ Ⓓ Ⓔ	14	Ⓐ Ⓑ Ⓒ Ⓓ Ⓔ	24	Ⓐ Ⓑ Ⓒ Ⓓ Ⓔ
5	Ⓐ Ⓑ Ⓒ Ⓓ Ⓔ	15	Ⓐ Ⓑ Ⓒ Ⓓ Ⓔ	25	Ⓐ Ⓑ Ⓒ Ⓓ Ⓔ
6	Ⓐ Ⓑ Ⓒ Ⓓ Ⓔ	16	Ⓐ Ⓑ Ⓒ Ⓓ Ⓔ	26	Ⓐ Ⓑ Ⓒ Ⓓ Ⓔ
7	Ⓐ Ⓑ Ⓒ Ⓓ Ⓔ	17	Ⓐ Ⓑ Ⓒ Ⓓ Ⓔ	27	Ⓐ Ⓑ Ⓒ Ⓓ Ⓔ
8	Ⓐ Ⓑ Ⓒ Ⓓ Ⓔ	18	Ⓐ Ⓑ Ⓒ Ⓓ Ⓔ	28	Ⓐ Ⓑ Ⓒ Ⓓ Ⓔ
9	Ⓐ Ⓑ Ⓒ Ⓓ Ⓔ	19	Ⓐ Ⓑ Ⓒ Ⓓ Ⓔ	29	Ⓐ Ⓑ Ⓒ Ⓓ Ⓔ
10	Ⓐ Ⓑ Ⓒ Ⓓ Ⓔ	20	Ⓐ Ⓑ Ⓒ Ⓓ Ⓔ	30	Ⓐ Ⓑ Ⓒ Ⓓ Ⓔ

1. In the following figure, the shaded squares are what fractional part of the whole set of squares?

    (A) $\frac{1}{2}$

    (B) $\frac{5}{8}$

    (C) $\frac{2}{3}$

    (D) $\frac{3}{5}$

    (E) $\frac{6}{11}$

2. Which of the following is greater than $\frac{12}{8}$?

    (A) $\frac{1}{2}$

    (B) $\frac{5}{2}$

    (C) $\frac{3}{4}$

    (D) 1

    (E) 1.4

3. If $\frac{1}{3}$ of a number is greater than 8, the number must be

    (A) Less than 4

    (B) Equal to 16

    (C) Equal to 24

    (D) Greater than 24

    (E) Equal to 32

4. If $4 \times (M + N) = 20$ and M is greater than 0, then N could Not be

    (A) 1

    (B) 2

    (C) 3

    (D) 4

    (E) 5

5. Which of the following is closest to 5.03?

    (A) 6

    (B) 5.5

    (C) 5

    (D) 5.4

    (E) 6.5

6. At a Zoo, the ratio of lions to tigers is 10 to 6. Which of the following could NOT be the total number of lions and tigers in the zoo?

    (A) 64

    (B) 80

    (C) 98

    (D) 104

    (E) 160

7. In the multiplication below, A represents which digit?
    $$14 \times 3A2 = 4,788$$

    (A) 2

    (B) 3

    (C) 4

    (D) 6

    (E) 8

8. If N is an even number, which of the following is always an odd number?

    (A) $\frac{N}{2}$

    (B) $N + 4$

    (C) $2N$

    (D) $(2 \times N) + 2$

    (E) $N + 1$

9. $8.9 - 4.08$ is closest to which of the following.

(A) 4.1

(B) 4.8

(C) 6

(D) 8

(E) 13

$$x = 2{,}456, y = 259$$

10. Numbers x and y are shown above. How many times larger is the value of digit 5 in the number x, than the value of digit 5 in the number y?

(A) 1

(B) 10

(C) 100

(D) 1,000

(E) 10,000

11. If 5 added to a number, the sum is 20. If the same number added to 25, the answer is

(A) 30

(B) 35

(C) 40

(D) 45

(E) 50

12. $\dfrac{2+5+6\times1+1}{3+5} =?$

(A) $\dfrac{15}{8}$

(B) $\dfrac{4}{8}$

(C) $\dfrac{7}{4}$

(D) $\dfrac{6}{8}$

(E) $\dfrac{10}{8}$

13. What is the Area of the square shown in the following square?

(A) 2

(B) 4

(C) 6

(D) 8

(E) 10

14. If 20 is the product of 4 and x, then 20 can be divided by which of the following?

(A) $x + 4$

(B) $2x - 4$

(C) $x - 2$

(D) $x \times 4$

(E) $x + 1$

15. Use the equations below to answer the question:

$$x + 12 = 18$$
$$16 + y = 21$$

What is the value of $x + y$?

(A) 9

(B) 10

(C) 11

(D) 12

(E) 14

16. Which of the following expressions has the same value as $\frac{5}{4} \times \frac{6}{2}$?

(A) $\frac{6 \times 3}{4}$

(B) $\frac{6 \times 2}{4}$

(C) $\frac{5 \times 6}{4}$

(D) $\frac{5 \times 3}{4}$

(E) $\frac{8 \times 3}{4}$

17. When 5 is added to three times number N, the result is 41. Then N is

(A) 11

(B) 12

(C) 14

(D) 16

(E) 18

18. At noon, the temperature was 15 degrees. By midnight, it had dropped another 20 degrees. What was the temperature at midnight?

    (A) 10 degrees above zero

    (B) 10 degrees below zero

    (C) 5 degrees above zero

    (D) 5 degrees below zero

    (E) 15 degrees below zero

19. If a triangle has a base of 5 cm and a height of 8 cm, what is the area of the triangle?

    (A) $15cm^2$

    (B) $20cm^2$

    (C) $40cm^2$

    (D) $45cm^2$

    (E) $50cm^2$

20. Which formula would you use to find the area of a square?

    (A) $length \times width \times height$

    (B) $\frac{1}{2} base \times height$

    (C) $length \times width$

    (D) $side \times side$

    (E) $\frac{1}{2}(length \times width \times heigt)$

21. What is the next number in this sequence? $2, 5, 9, 14, 20, ...$?

    (A) 27

    (B) 26

    (C) 25

    (D) 21

    (E) 20

22. What is the average of the following numbers? 6, 10, 12, 23, 45

    (A) 19

    (B) 19.2

    (C) 19.5

    (D) 20

    (E) 25

23. If there are 8 red balls and 12 blue balls in a basket, what is the probability that John will pick out a red ball from the basket?

    (A) $\frac{18}{10}$

    (B) $\frac{2}{5}$

    (C) $\frac{2}{10}$

    (D) $\frac{3}{5}$

    (E) $\frac{20}{10}$

24. How many lines of symmetry does an equilateral triangle have?

    (A) 5

    (B) 4

    (C) 3

    (D) 2

    (E) 1

25. What is 10% of 200?

    (A) 10

    (B) 20

    (C) 30

    (D) 40

    (E) 50

26. Which of the following statement is False?

   (A) $2 \times 2 = 4$

   (B) $(4 + 1) \times 5 = 25$

   (C) $6 \div (3 - 1) = 1$

   (D) $6 \times (4 - 2) = 12$

   (E) $(10 + 23) \times 10 = 330$

27. If all the sides in the following figure are of equal length and length of one side is 4, what is the perimeter of the figure?

   (A) 15

   (B) 18

   (C) 20

   (D) 24

   (E) 28

28. $\dfrac{4}{5} - \dfrac{3}{5} = ?$

   (A) 0.3

   (B) 0.35

   (C) 0.2

   (D) 0.25

   (E) 0.1

29. If $N = 2$ and $\dfrac{64}{N} + 4 = \square$, then $\square =$

   (A) 30

   (B) 32

   (C) 34

   (D) 36

   (E) 38

30. Four people can paint 4 houses in 10 days. How many people are needed to paint 8 houses in 5 days?

   (A) 6

   (B) 8

   (C) 12

   (D) 16

   (E) 20

End of SSAT Lower Level Math Practice Test 1

SSAT Lower Level Math

Practice Test 2

2020 - 2021

Total number of questions: 30

Total time for this test: 30 Minutes

Calculator is NOT permitted for SSAT Lower Level Math Test.

13

SSAT Lower Level Mathematics Practice Test Answer Sheet

Remove (or photocopy) this answer sheet and use it to complete the practice test.

SSAT Lower Level Mathematics Practice Test Answer Sheet

SSAT Lower Level Practice Test 2

1	Ⓐ Ⓑ Ⓒ Ⓓ Ⓔ	11 Ⓐ Ⓑ Ⓒ Ⓓ Ⓔ	21 Ⓐ Ⓑ Ⓒ Ⓓ Ⓔ
2	Ⓐ Ⓑ Ⓒ Ⓓ Ⓔ	12 Ⓐ Ⓑ Ⓒ Ⓓ Ⓔ	22 Ⓐ Ⓑ Ⓒ Ⓓ Ⓔ
3	Ⓐ Ⓑ Ⓒ Ⓓ Ⓔ	13 Ⓐ Ⓑ Ⓒ Ⓓ Ⓔ	23 Ⓐ Ⓑ Ⓒ Ⓓ Ⓔ
4	Ⓐ Ⓑ Ⓒ Ⓓ Ⓔ	14 Ⓐ Ⓑ Ⓒ Ⓓ Ⓔ	24 Ⓐ Ⓑ Ⓒ Ⓓ Ⓔ
5	Ⓐ Ⓑ Ⓒ Ⓓ Ⓔ	15 Ⓐ Ⓑ Ⓒ Ⓓ Ⓔ	25 Ⓐ Ⓑ Ⓒ Ⓓ Ⓔ
6	Ⓐ Ⓑ Ⓒ Ⓓ Ⓔ	16 Ⓐ Ⓑ Ⓒ Ⓓ Ⓔ	26 Ⓐ Ⓑ Ⓒ Ⓓ Ⓔ
7	Ⓐ Ⓑ Ⓒ Ⓓ Ⓔ	17 Ⓐ Ⓑ Ⓒ Ⓓ Ⓔ	27 Ⓐ Ⓑ Ⓒ Ⓓ Ⓔ
8	Ⓐ Ⓑ Ⓒ Ⓓ Ⓔ	18 Ⓐ Ⓑ Ⓒ Ⓓ Ⓔ	28 Ⓐ Ⓑ Ⓒ Ⓓ Ⓔ
9	Ⓐ Ⓑ Ⓒ Ⓓ Ⓔ	19 Ⓐ Ⓑ Ⓒ Ⓓ Ⓔ	29 Ⓐ Ⓑ Ⓒ Ⓓ Ⓔ
10	Ⓐ Ⓑ Ⓒ Ⓓ Ⓔ	20 Ⓐ Ⓑ Ⓒ Ⓓ Ⓔ	30 Ⓐ Ⓑ Ⓒ Ⓓ Ⓔ

1. $\frac{8}{2} - \frac{3}{2} = ?$

   (A) 1

   (B) 1.5

   (C) 2

   (D) 2.5

   (E) 3

2. If $48 = 3 \times N + 12$, then $N =$

   (A) 8

   (B) 12

   (C) 14

   (D) 15

   (E) 20

3. The area of each square in the following shape is $8 \ cm^2$. What is the area of shaded squares?

   (A) $40 \ cm^2$

   (B) $42 cm^2$

   (C) $44 cm^2$

   (D) $45 cm^2$

   (E) $46 cm^2$

4. What is the value of x in the following math equation?
   $$\frac{x}{15} + 9 = 11$$

   (A) 15

   (B) 20

   (C) 25

   (D) 28

   (E) 30

5. When 3 is added to four times a number N, the result is 23. Which of the following equations represents this statement?

(A) $4 + 3N = 23$

(B) $23N + 4 = 3$

(C) $4N + 3 = 23$

(D) $4N + 23 = 3$

(E) $3N + 23 = 4$

6. When 78 is divided by 5, the remainder is the same as when 45 is divided by

(A) 2

(B) 4

(C) 5

(D) 7

(E) 9

7. John has 2,400 cards and Max has 606 cards. How many more cards does John have than Max?

(A) 1,794

(B) 1,798

(C) 1,812

(D) 1,828

(E) 1,994

8. In the following right triangle, what is the value of x?

(A) 15

(B) 30

(C) 45

(D) 60

(E) It cannot be determined from the information given

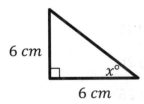

9. What is 5 percent of 480?

    (A) 20

    (B) 24

    (C) 30

    (D) 40

    (E) 44

10. In a basket, the ratio of red marbles to blue marbles is 3 to 2. Which of the following could NOT be the total number of red and blue marbles in the basket?

    (A) 15

    (B) 32

    (C) 55

    (D) 60

    (E) 70

11. A square has an area of $81\ cm^2$. What is its perimeter?

    (A) $28\ cm$

    (B) $32\ cm$

    (C) $34\ cm$

    (D) $36\ cm$

    (E) $54\ cm$

12. Find the missing number in the sequence? $39, 41, 44, \ldots, 53$

    (A) 45

    (B) 46

    (C) 47

    (D) 48

    (E) 49

13. The length of a rectangle is 3 times of its width. If the length is 18, what is the perimeter of the rectangle?

(A) 24

(B) 30

(C) 36

(D) 48

(E) 56

14. Mary has y dollars. John has \$10 more than Mary. If John gives Mary \$12, then in terms of y, how much does John have now?

(A) $y + 1$

(B) $y + 10$

(C) $y - 2$

(D) $y - 1$

(E) $y + 3$

15. Dividing 107 by 6 leaves a remainder of

(A) 1

(B) 2

(C) 3

(D) 4

(E) 5

16. If $6,000 + A - 200 = 7,400$, then $A =$

(A) 200

(B) 600

(C) 1,600

(D) 2,200

(E) 3,000

17. For what price is 15 percent off the same as $75 off?

   (A) $200

   (B) $300

   (C) $350

   (D) $400

   (E) $500

Use this diagram to answer the question.

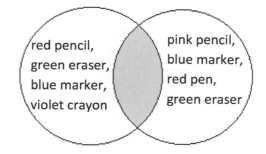

18. What thing could be found in the shaded part of this diagram?

   (A) Red pen

   (B) Blue marker

   (C) Green eraser

   (D) Violet crayon

   (E) Violet crayon and green eraser

19. Use the equation below to answer the question.
$$x + 3 = 6$$
$$2y = 8$$

   What is the value of $y - x$?

   (A) 1

   (B) 2

   (C) 3

   (D) 4

   (E) 5

20. If $310 - x + 116 = 225$, then $x =$

(A) 101

(B) 156

(C) 201

(D) 211

(E) 310

21. $2\frac{1}{2} + 3\frac{1}{2} + 1\frac{1}{2}$ is equal to

(A) 1

(B) 2

(C) $4\frac{1}{2}$

(D) 7

(E) $7\frac{1}{2}$

22. Solve:
$8.08 - 5.6 =$

(A) 2.42

(B) 2.46

(C) 2.48

(D) 3

(E) 3.2

23. If $500 + \square - 180 = 1{,}100$, then $\square = ?$

(A) 580

(B) 660

(C) 700

(D) 780

(E) 900

24. There are 60 students in a class. If the ratio of the number of girls to the total number of students in the class is $\frac{1}{6}$, which are the following is the number of boys in that class?

   (A) 10

   (B) 20

   (C) 25

   (D) 40

   (E) 50

25. If $N \times (5 - 3) = 12$ then $N =$?

   (A) 6

   (B) 12

   (C) 13

   (D) 14

   (E) 18

26. If $x \blacksquare y = 3x + y - 2$, what is the value of $4 \blacksquare 12$?

   (A) 4

   (B) 18

   (C) 22

   (D) 36

   (E) 48

27. Of the following, which number if the greatest?

   (A) 0.092

   (B) 0.8913

   (C) 0.8923

   (D) 0.8896

   (E) 0.88

28. $\frac{7}{8} - \frac{3}{4} =$

   (A) 0.125

   (B) 0.375

   (C) 0.5

   (D) 0.625

   (E) 0.775

29. Which of the following is the closest to 4.02?

   (A) 4

   (B) 4.2

   (C) 4.3

   (D) 4.4

   (E) 4.5

30. Which of the following statements is False?

   (A) $(7 \times 2 + 14) \times 2 = 56$

   (B) $(2 \times 5 + 4) \div 2 = 7$

   (C) $3 + (3 \times 6) = 21$

   (D) $4 \times (3 + 9) = 48$

   (E) $14 \div (2 + 5) = 5$

End of SSAT Lower Level Math Practice Test 2

SSAT Lower Level Math

Practice Test 3

2020 - 2021

Total number of questions: 30

Total time for this test: 30 Minutes

Calculator is NOT permitted for SSAT Lower Level Math Test.

25

SSAT Lower Level Mathematics Practice Test Answer Sheet

Remove (or photocopy) this answer sheet and use it to complete the practice test.

SSAT Lower Level Mathematics Practice Test Answer Sheet

SSAT Lower Level Practice Test 3

1	Ⓐ Ⓑ Ⓒ Ⓓ Ⓔ	11	Ⓐ Ⓑ Ⓒ Ⓓ Ⓔ	21	Ⓐ Ⓑ Ⓒ Ⓓ Ⓔ
2	Ⓐ Ⓑ Ⓒ Ⓓ Ⓔ	12	Ⓐ Ⓑ Ⓒ Ⓓ Ⓔ	22	Ⓐ Ⓑ Ⓒ Ⓓ Ⓔ
3	Ⓐ Ⓑ Ⓒ Ⓓ Ⓔ	13	Ⓐ Ⓑ Ⓒ Ⓓ Ⓔ	23	Ⓐ Ⓑ Ⓒ Ⓓ Ⓔ
4	Ⓐ Ⓑ Ⓒ Ⓓ Ⓔ	14	Ⓐ Ⓑ Ⓒ Ⓓ Ⓔ	24	Ⓐ Ⓑ Ⓒ Ⓓ Ⓔ
5	Ⓐ Ⓑ Ⓒ Ⓓ Ⓔ	15	Ⓐ Ⓑ Ⓒ Ⓓ Ⓔ	25	Ⓐ Ⓑ Ⓒ Ⓓ Ⓔ
6	Ⓐ Ⓑ Ⓒ Ⓓ Ⓔ	16	Ⓐ Ⓑ Ⓒ Ⓓ Ⓔ	26	Ⓐ Ⓑ Ⓒ Ⓓ Ⓔ
7	Ⓐ Ⓑ Ⓒ Ⓓ Ⓔ	17	Ⓐ Ⓑ Ⓒ Ⓓ Ⓔ	27	Ⓐ Ⓑ Ⓒ Ⓓ Ⓔ
8	Ⓐ Ⓑ Ⓒ Ⓓ Ⓔ	18	Ⓐ Ⓑ Ⓒ Ⓓ Ⓔ	28	Ⓐ Ⓑ Ⓒ Ⓓ Ⓔ
9	Ⓐ Ⓑ Ⓒ Ⓓ Ⓔ	19	Ⓐ Ⓑ Ⓒ Ⓓ Ⓔ	29	Ⓐ Ⓑ Ⓒ Ⓓ Ⓔ
10	Ⓐ Ⓑ Ⓒ Ⓓ Ⓔ	20	Ⓐ Ⓑ Ⓒ Ⓓ Ⓔ	30	Ⓐ Ⓑ Ⓒ Ⓓ Ⓔ

1. Mia twirls her hair once every 12 seconds. How many times does she twirl her hair in a minute?

    (A) 5

    (B) 6

    (C) 7

    (D) 10

    (E) 12

2. If $\frac{2}{8} = \frac{\blacksquare}{56}$, then $\blacksquare = ?$

    (A) 7

    (B) 8

    (C) 9

    (D) 14

    (E) 16

3. What is the value of the "9" in 851.951?

    (A) 9 tenth

    (B) 9 hundredths

    (C) 9 tens

    (D) 9 thousandths

    (E) 9 ones

4. $\dfrac{3 \times (6+5)}{33} = ?$

   (A) 1

   (B) 1.75

   (C) 2

   (D) 2.25

   (E) 4.75

5. If $x + 2y - 12 = y$, then $x + y =$

   (A) 6

   (B) 8

   (C) 12

   (D) 15

   (E) 18

6. Use the pattern to help answer the question.

$$1 + 3 = 2^2$$
$$1 + 3 + 5 = 3^2$$
$$1 + 3 + 5 + 7 = 4^2$$

   What is the solution to $1 + 3 + 5 + 7 + 9 + 11 + 13 + 15 + 17$?

   (A) 6^2

   (B) 7^2

   (C) 8^2

   (D) 9^2

   (E) 15^2

7. In the multiplication below, B represents which digit?
$$15 \times 4B5 = 6{,}375$$

(A) 2

(B) 3

(C) 4

(D) 6

(E) 8

8. If N is an odd, which of the following is always an even number?

(A) $(2 \times N) + 1$

(B) $N + 2$

(C) $3N$

(D) $(3 \times N) + 2$

(E) $2N$

9. $9.5 - 5.08$ is closest to which of the following.

(A) 4.1

(B) 4.4

(C) 4.8

(D) 9

(E) 14

10. What fraction of the following shape is shaded?

(A) $\frac{1}{3}$

(B) $\frac{2}{3}$

(C) $\frac{4}{9}$

(D) $\frac{3}{5}$

(E) $\frac{5}{9}$

11. A notebook costs $2.15 and Anna wants to purchase 186 notebooks. Which expression gives the best estimate of the total cost of Anna's purchase in dollars?

(A) 2×20

(B) 2×200

(C) 20×190

(D) 20×290

(E) 20×100

12. In the following diagram, the shaded region shows people who drink …

(A) hot chocolate and green tea

(B) green tea and orange juice

(C) orange juice and hot chocolate

(D) hot chocolate, green tea and orange juice
(E) hot chocolate

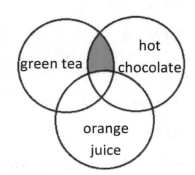

13. What is the Area of the rectangle shown below?

(A) 3

(B) 4

(C) 6

(D) 9

(E) 12

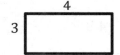

14. Which of the following shows a line of symmetry?

(A)

(B)

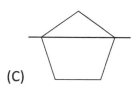

(C)

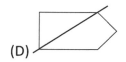

(D)

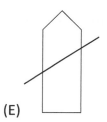

(E)

Use the equations below to answer the question:
$$x + 3 = 9$$
$$19 + y = 25$$

15. What is the value of $x - y$?

(A) 0

(B) 6

(C) 10

(D) 12

(E) 18

16. Which of the following expressions has the same value as $\frac{2}{5} \times \frac{10}{4}$?

   (A) $\frac{2 \times 4}{4}$

   (B) $\frac{2 \times 5}{20}$

   (C) $\frac{5 \times 6}{4}$

   (D) $\frac{5 \times 4}{20}$

   (E) $\frac{8 \times 3}{4}$

17. When 8 is added to five times number A, the result is 83. Then A is

   (A) 10

   (B) 15

   (C) 20

   (D) 30

   (E) 32

18. Mike read 3 pages of a story book in 42 minutes. At the same rate of speed, how long would he need in order to read 25 pages?

   (A) 75 minutes

   (B) 126 minutes

   (C) 258 minutes

   (D) 350 minutes

   (E) 387 minutes

19. Number A is shown in the following diagram. Which of the following is equal to $A - 2.3$?

   (A) 1.9

   (B) 2.1

   (C) 3.4

   (D) 3.7

   (E) 4.4

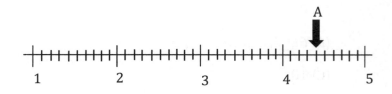

20. Which formula would you use to find the area of a triangle?

    (A) $length \times width \times height$

    (B) $\frac{1}{2} \times base \times height$

    (C) $length \times width$

    (D) $side \times side$

    (E) $\frac{1}{2}(length \times width \times heigt)$

21. What is the next number in this sequence? $3, 6, 10, 15, 21, \ldots$

    (A) 28

    (B) 26

    (C) 24

    (D) 21

    (E) 20

22. Which of the following shapes can be folded to create a Cone?

(A)

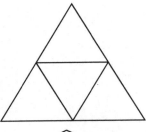

(B)

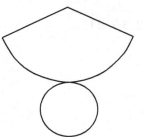

(C)

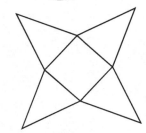

(D)

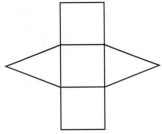

(E)

23. According to the following graph, how many buses were sold?

400 VEHICLE WERE SOLD

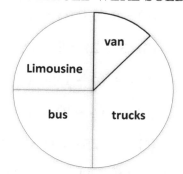

   (A) 50

   (B) 100

   (C) 150

   (D) 200

   (E) 250

24. The perimeter of a square is 60 cm. What is its area?

   (A) 60 cm^2

   (B) 90 cm^2

   (C) 120 cm^2

   (D) 225 cm^2

   (E) 400 cm^2

25. What is 10% of 300?

   (A) 20

   (B) 30

   (C) 40

   (D) 50

   (E) 60

26. Which of the following statement is False?

    (A) $3 \times (5 - 2) = 9$

    (B) $(3 + 2) \times 5 = 25$

    (C) $6 \div (4 - 1) = 1$

    (D) $6 \times (4 - 2) = 12$

    (E) $(8 + 25) \times 10 = 330$

27. If all the sides in the following polygon are of equal length and its perimeter is 72, what is the length of one side?

    (A) 5

    (B) 6

    (C) 7

    (D) 8

    (E) 9

28. $\frac{4}{5} - \frac{2}{5} = ?$

    (A) 0.3

    (B) 0.35

    (C) 0.4

    (D) 0.45

    (E) 0.5

29. If $C = 8$ and $19 - (56 \div C) - 8 = \square$, then $\square =$

    (A) 3

    (B) 4

    (C) 5

    (D) 7

    (E) 8

30. Oliver, Tom, and Stevie were driving at the same speed. It took Oliver 16 minutes to drive 32 miles. How long did it take Tom to drive 52 miles?

(A) 22

(B) 24

(C) 26

(D) 28

(E) 34

End of SSAT Lower Level Math Practice Test 3

SSAT Lower Level Math

Practice Test 4

2020 - 2021

Total number of questions: 30

Total time for this test: 30 Minutes

Calculator is NOT permitted for SSAT Lower Level Math Test.

39

SSAT Lower Level Mathematics Practice Test Answer Sheet

Remove (or photocopy) this answer sheet and use it to complete the practice test.

SSAT Lower Level Practice Test 4

SSAT Lower Level Mathematics Practice Test Answer Sheet

1	A B C D E	11	A B C D E	21	A B C D E
2	A B C D E	12	A B C D E	22	A B C D E
3	A B C D E	13	A B C D E	23	A B C D E
4	A B C D E	14	A B C D E	24	A B C D E
5	A B C D E	15	A B C D E	25	A B C D E
6	A B C D E	16	A B C D E	26	A B C D E
7	A B C D E	17	A B C D E	27	A B C D E
8	A B C D E	18	A B C D E	28	A B C D E
9	A B C D E	19	A B C D E	29	A B C D E
10	A B C D E	20	A B C D E	30	A B C D E

1. $\frac{8}{2} - \frac{5}{2} = ?$

   (A) 0.2

   (B) 0.3

   (C) 0.4

   (D) 1

   (E) 1.5

2. If $48 = 2 \times A + 10$, then $A =$

   (A) 10

   (B) 19

   (C) 24

   (D) 25

   (E) 28

3. When folded, what will the shape in the following figure become?

   (A) Cylinder

   (B) Sphere

   (C) Cube

   (D) Square pyramid

   (E) Cone

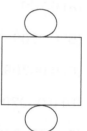

4. P is a whole number between 3 and 7. P is also between 5 and 8. Which is P?

   (A) 3

   (B) 4

   (C) 5.5

   (D) 6

   (E) 7

5. If $x = 5$, which of these statements is false?

(A) $x + 16 = 45 - 24$

(B) $11 - x = 5 + 1$

(C) $x + 26 = 16 + 17$

(D) $x - 1 = 27 - 23$

(E) $51 - 27 = 19 + x$

6. If Emma ran 4 miles in half an hour, her average speed was

(A) 2 miles per hour

(B) 4 miles per hour

(C) 5.5 miles per hour

(D) 8 miles per hour

(E) 12 miles per hour

7. Which of the fallowing is the biggest?

(A) 0.709

(B) 0.0709

(C) 0.00709

(D) 0.000709

(E) 0.0000709

8. In a grocery cart, there is an equal number of snacks and desserts. How many items could be in the cart?

(A) 15

(B) 17

(C) 28

(D) 31

(E) 33

9. What fraction of the following shape is shaded??

    (A) $\frac{1}{3}$

    (B) $\frac{2}{3}$

    (C) $\frac{1}{2}$

    (D) $\frac{5}{6}$

    (E) $\frac{2}{5}$

10. If the shaded section of the circle in this figure signifies 350 types of birds, how many birds could the unshaded section represent?

    (A) 270

    (B) 370

    (C) 390

    (D) 450

    (E) 510

11. According to the following graph, how many more cars did John's sell in 2015 than in 2013?

    (A) 100

    (B) 200

    (C) 250

    (D) 400

    (E) 500

John's Annual TV Sales

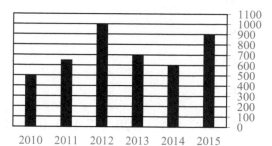

12. What is the value of the "2" in 961.582

    (A) 2 tenth

    (B) 2 hundredth

    (C) 2 tents

    (D) 2 thousandths

    (E) 2 ones

13. The diameter of the semicircle in the following figure is 18 *cm*. What is its radius? Note: The radius is the length halfway across the circle.

   (A) 3

   (B) 6

   (C) 8

   (D) 9

   (E) 10

14. James bought some movie tickets for $27.45. He paid with a 50 dollar bill. How much change did he receive?

   (A) 20.65

   (B) 21.25

   (C) 22.55

   (D) 23.45

   (E) 26.45

15. Dividing 150 by 4 leaves a remainder of

   (A) 1

   (B) 2

   (C) 3

   (D) 4

   (E) 5

16. If $5,000 + A - 200 = 7,400$, then $A =$

   (A) 200

   (B) 1600

   (C) 2,600

   (D) 3,200

   (E) 3,400

17. What is 16 percent of 250?

   (A) 10

   (B) 16

   (C) 20

   (D) 40

   (E) 50

18. Which of the following numbers is less than $\frac{5}{2}$?

   (A) 1.07

   (B) $\frac{7}{2}$

   (C) 2.8

   (D) 3

   (E) 3.5

19. Use the equation below to answer the question.

$$\frac{x}{2} - 2 = 6$$
$$2y + 4 = 20$$

What is the value of $x - 2y$?

   (A) 0

   (B) 2

   (C) 4

   (D) 16

   (E) 32

20. If $125 - y + 16 = 17$, then $y =$

   (A) 92

   (B) 123

   (C) 124

   (D) 156

   (E) 158

21. Of the following, 25 percent of $53.99 is closest to

    (A) $9.90

    (B) $10.00

    (C) $13.50

    (D) $14.50

    (E) $15.00

22. Solve: $\frac{9}{20} - \frac{7}{20} =$

    (A) 0.1

    (B) 0.2

    (C) 0.02

    (D) 0.025

    (E) 0.79

23. If $1,200 - \Box + \frac{1,800}{2} = 400 + 700$, then $\Box =$

    (A) 1,000

    (B) 1,800

    (C) 1,900

    (D) 2,400

    (E) 3,200

24. In 12 hours, Sophia's poppy sleeps $\frac{3}{4}$ of the time. How many hours does the poppy sleep?

    (A) 1 hours

    (B) 3 hours

    (C) 6 hours

    (D) 8 hours

    (E) 9 hours

25. If $N \times (5 - 2) = 12$ then $N =$?

   (A) 4

   (B) 12

   (C) 13

   (D) 14

   (E) 20

26. For any numbers a and b, $a \blacklozenge b = 2a - b$. What is the value of $1 \blacklozenge 4$?

   (A) 0

   (B) 2

   (C) -4

   (D) -2

   (E) -4

27. Of the following, which number is the greatest?

   (A) 0.096

   (B) 0.9913

   (C) 0.9923

   (D) 0.9896

   (E) 0.98

28. $\dfrac{7}{10} + \dfrac{1}{2} =$

   (A) 0.1

   (B) 0.2

   (C) 0.5

   (D) 0.75

   (E) 1.2

29. Which of the following is the closest to 125.02?

   (A) 125

   (B) 125.2

   (C) 1255.3

   (D) 125.5

   (E) 126

30. Which of the following statements is False?

   (A) $(4 \times 2 + 3) \times 2 = (2 \times 6 + 10)$

   (B) $(2 \times 5 + 4) = (7 + 3 \times 2)$

   (C) $(4 \times 7) \div 2 = (24 \div 2) + 2$

   (D) $4 \times (3 + 8) = (19 + 25)$

   (E) $(2 \times 7 + 1) \div 3 = (6 \times 5) \div 6$

End of SSAT Lower Level Math Practice Test 4

SSAT Lower Level Math

Practice Test 5

2020 - 2021

Total number of questions: 30

Total time for this test: 30 Minutes

Calculator is NOT permitted for SSAT Lower Level Math Test.

49

SSAT Lower Level Mathematics Practice Test Answer Sheet

Remove (or photocopy) this answer sheet and use it to complete the practice test.

SSAT Lower Level Mathematics Practice Test Answer Sheet

SSAT Lower Level Practice Test 5

1	Ⓐ Ⓑ Ⓒ Ⓓ Ⓔ	11	Ⓐ Ⓑ Ⓒ Ⓓ Ⓔ	21	Ⓐ Ⓑ Ⓒ Ⓓ Ⓔ
2	Ⓐ Ⓑ Ⓒ Ⓓ Ⓔ	12	Ⓐ Ⓑ Ⓒ Ⓓ Ⓔ	22	Ⓐ Ⓑ Ⓒ Ⓓ Ⓔ
3	Ⓐ Ⓑ Ⓒ Ⓓ Ⓔ	13	Ⓐ Ⓑ Ⓒ Ⓓ Ⓔ	23	Ⓐ Ⓑ Ⓒ Ⓓ Ⓔ
4	Ⓐ Ⓑ Ⓒ Ⓓ Ⓔ	14	Ⓐ Ⓑ Ⓒ Ⓓ Ⓔ	24	Ⓐ Ⓑ Ⓒ Ⓓ Ⓔ
5	Ⓐ Ⓑ Ⓒ Ⓓ Ⓔ	15	Ⓐ Ⓑ Ⓒ Ⓓ Ⓔ	25	Ⓐ Ⓑ Ⓒ Ⓓ Ⓔ
6	Ⓐ Ⓑ Ⓒ Ⓓ Ⓔ	16	Ⓐ Ⓑ Ⓒ Ⓓ Ⓔ	26	Ⓐ Ⓑ Ⓒ Ⓓ Ⓔ
7	Ⓐ Ⓑ Ⓒ Ⓓ Ⓔ	17	Ⓐ Ⓑ Ⓒ Ⓓ Ⓔ	27	Ⓐ Ⓑ Ⓒ Ⓓ Ⓔ
8	Ⓐ Ⓑ Ⓒ Ⓓ Ⓔ	18	Ⓐ Ⓑ Ⓒ Ⓓ Ⓔ	28	Ⓐ Ⓑ Ⓒ Ⓓ Ⓔ
9	Ⓐ Ⓑ Ⓒ Ⓓ Ⓔ	19	Ⓐ Ⓑ Ⓒ Ⓓ Ⓔ	29	Ⓐ Ⓑ Ⓒ Ⓓ Ⓔ
10	Ⓐ Ⓑ Ⓒ Ⓓ Ⓔ	20	Ⓐ Ⓑ Ⓒ Ⓓ Ⓔ	30	Ⓐ Ⓑ Ⓒ Ⓓ Ⓔ

1. $\frac{8}{3} - \frac{4}{3} = ?$

   (A) 0.2

   (B) 0.3

   (C) 0.5

   (D) 0.6

   (E) $1\frac{1}{3}$

2. If $58 = 3 \times \Delta + 10$, then $\Delta =$

   (A) 10

   (B) 16

   (C) 24

   (D) 25

   (E) 28

3. If $a = b + 2c$ and $b = c$, then

   (A) $a = 3c$

   (B) $a = c$

   (C) $a - b = c$

   (D) $ab = c$

   (E) $a = b = c$

4. What is the value of y in the following math equation?
   $$8 = y - 12$$

   (A) 4

   (B) 20

   (C) 40

   (D) 50

   (E) 600

5. $550 - 200P =$

    (A) $350P$

    (B) $750P$

    (C) $3,500P$

    (D) $110,000P$

    (E) The answer cannot be determined from the information given.

6. Which of the following is NOT equal to a whole number?

    (A) $30 \times \frac{2}{3}$

    (B) $3 + 9$

    (C) $\frac{104}{4}$

    (D) $\frac{1}{6} \times 9$

    (E) $19.5 + 3.5$

7. The record for the 200-yard dash was 17.21 seconds. Maria beat the record by a twentieth of a second. What was Maria's time?

    (A) 17.01

    (B) 17.12

    (C) 17.16

    (D) 17.19

    (E) 17.20

8. Which transformation has been applied to the following shape?

    (A) A turn

    (B) A slide

    (C) A reflection

    (D) A slide followed by a turn

    (E) Rotate 90 degrees

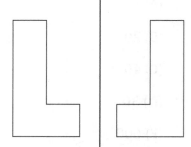

9. What is 5 percent of 360?

   (A) 15

   (B) 18

   (C) 35

   (D) 40

   (E) 44.5

10. Sophia types 2,880 words per hour. How many words does she type per minute?

    (A) 28

    (B) 42

    (C) 48

    (D) 52

    (E) 61

11. What is the value of α in figure below?

    (A) 55

    (B) 125

    (C) 145

    (D) 150

    (E) 155

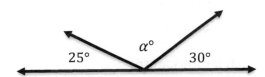

12. What is the missing number in the pattern in the following table?

    (A) 17.5

    (B) 21.5

    (C) 24

    (D) 26

    (E) 28

−2.5	10
1.5	14
5.5	18
9.5	22
13.5	?

13. 4 cubed is the same as

   (A) 4×4

   (B) $4 \times 4 \times 4 \times 4$

   (C) 12

   (D) 64

   (E) 256

14. James is five times the age of his 7-year-old daughter. How old is James?

   (A) 30

   (B) 33

   (C) 35

   (D) 42

   (E) 49

15. What is the value of the "8" in 962.581?

   (A) 8 tenth

   (B) 8 hundredths

   (C) 8 tens

   (D) 8 thousandths

   (E) 8 ones

16. If $2,500 = 600 + C - 1,900$, then $C =$

   (A) 0

   (B) 1200

   (C) 2,900

   (D) 3,800

   (E) 5,000

17. When folded, what will the shape in the following figure become?

    (A) tetrahedron

    (B) cone

    (C) square pyramid

    (D) cylinder

    (E) triangular prism

18. Which of the following numbers is less than $\frac{7}{2}$?

    (A) 2.4

    (B) $\frac{9}{2}$

    (C) 3.8

    (D) 4.8

    (E) 4.5

19. Use the equation below to answer the question.
$$x - 8 = 7$$
$$y - 7 = 9$$
    What is the value of $2 \times y - 2 \times x$?

    (A) 1

    (B) 2

    (C) 3

    (D) 4

    (E) 5

20. If $250 - 2y + 30 = 230$, then $y =$

    (A) 0

    (B) 20

    (C) 25

    (D) 50

    (E) 255

21. If $50 + n = 50$, then $50 \times n =$

(A) 0

(B) 1

(C) 50

(D) 100

(E) 2,500

22. Solve:
$12.58 + 5.5 - 2.85 =$

(A) 9.73

(B) 11.05

(C) 15.23

(D) 18.08

(E) 20.93

23. If $\square - \left(\frac{500}{2}\right) + (2 \times 300) = \left(\frac{1,800}{2}\right)$, then $\square =$?

(A) 200

(B) 450

(C) 550

(D) 850

(E) 1,750

24. What are the coordinates of point D in the figure?

(A) $(2, -2)$

(B) $(6, 1)$

(C) $(4, 3)$

(D) $(6, 9)$

(E) $(6, -1)$

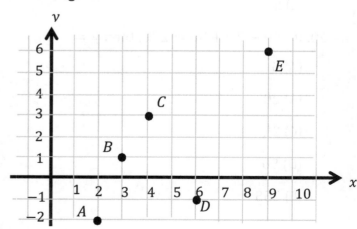

25. What fraction of the following shape is shaded?

    (A) $\frac{1}{3}$

    (B) $\frac{2}{5}$

    (C) $\frac{1}{2}$

    (D) $\frac{9}{17}$

    (E) $\frac{3}{10}$

26. $128.89 = ?$

    (A) $128 + \frac{7}{10} + \frac{9}{100} + \frac{5}{1,000}$

    (B) $128 + \frac{6}{10} + \frac{8}{100}$

    (C) $128 + \frac{6}{100} + \frac{8}{10} + \frac{3}{100}$

    (D) $128 + \frac{89}{10}$

    (E) $128 + \frac{9}{1,000} + \frac{8}{100}$

27. Of the following, which number if the greatest?

    (A) 0.076

    (B) 0.7913

    (C) 0.7923

    (D) 0.7896

    (E) 0.78

28. $\frac{20}{8} - \frac{1}{2} - \frac{2}{4} =$

    (A) 1.2

    (B) 1.5

    (C) 2.5

    (D) 4.5

    (E) 8.5

29. Which of the following is the closest to 7.06?

   (A) 7

   (B) 7.2

   (C) 7.3

   (D) 7.5

   (E) 8

30. Which of the following statements is False?

   (A) $(\frac{1}{2} \times 10) = (\frac{1}{4} \times 20)$

   (B) $(9 + 7 + 8) = (2 \times 4 \times 3)$

   (C) $(\frac{6}{2} \times \frac{2}{3}) = (\frac{4}{3} \times \frac{6}{4})$

   (D) $(3 \times 5 \times 2) = (\frac{6}{2} \times 10)$

   (E) $(\frac{8}{2} \times \frac{5}{2}) = (4 \times 5)$

End of SSAT Lower Level Math Practice Test 5

SSAT Lower Level Math Practice Tests Answer Keys

Now, it's time to review your results to see where you went wrong and what areas you need to improve.

SSAT Lower Level Math Practice Test 1				SSAT Lower Level Math Practice Test 2				SSAT Lower Level Math Practice Test 3				SSAT Lower Level Math Practice Test 4			
1	D	21	A	1	D	21	E	1	A	21	A	1	E	21	C
2	B	22	B	2	B	22	C	2	D	22	B	2	B	22	A
3	D	23	B	3	A	23	D	3	A	23	B	3	A	23	A
4	E	24	C	4	E	24	E	4	A	24	D	4	D	24	E
5	C	25	B	5	C	25	A	5	C	25	B	5	C	25	A
6	C	26	C	6	D	26	C	6	D	26	C	6	D	26	D
7	C	27	D	7	A	27	C	7	A	27	E	7	A	27	C
8	E	28	C	8	C	28	A	8	E	28	C	8	C	28	E
9	B	29	D	9	B	29	A	9	B	29	B	9	A	29	A
10	A	30	D	10	B	30	E	10	C	30	C	10	A	30	B
11	C			11	D			11	B			11	B		
12	C			12	D			12	A			12	D		
13	B			13	D			13	E			13	D		
14	D			14	C			14	B			14	C		
15	C			15	E			15	A			15	B		
16	D			16	C			16	D			16	C		
17	B			17	E			17	B			17	D		
18	D			18	B			18	D			18	A		
19	B			19	A			19	B			19	A		
20	D			20	C			20	B			20	C		

SSAT Lower Level Math Practice Test 5			
1	E	21	A
2	B	22	C
3	A	23	C
4	B	24	E
5	E	25	C
6	D	26	C
7	C	27	C
8	C	28	B
9	B	29	A
10	C	30	E
11	B		
12	D		
13	D		
14	C		
15	B		
16	D		
17	C		
18	A		
19	B		
20	C		

Score Your Test

SSAT scores are broken down by its three sections: Verbal, Quantitative (or Math), and Reading. A sum of the three sections is also reported.

For the SSAT lower level, the score range is 300-600, the lowest possible score a student can earn is 300 and the highest score is 600 for each section. A student receives 1 point for every correct answer. For SSAT Lower Level, there is no penalty for wrong answers. That means that you can calculate the raw score by adding together the number of right answers.

The total scaled score for a Lower Level SSAT is the sum of the scores for the quantitative, verbal, and reading sections. A student will also receive a percentile score of between 1-99% that compares that student's test scores with those of other test takers of same grade and gender from the past 3 years.

Use the following table to convert SSAT Lower Level Quantitative Reasoning raw score to scaled score.

SSAT Lowe Level Quantitative Reasoning raw score to scaled score

Raw Scores	Scaled Scores
Below 10	*Below* 400
11 − 15	410 − 450
16 − 20	560 − 500
21 − 25	510 − 550
26 − 30	560 − 600

SSAT Lower Level Math Practice Tests Answers and Explanations

SSAT Lower Level Quantitative Practice Test 1

1. **Choice D is correct.**

There are 10 squares and 6 of them are shaded. Therefore, 6 out of 10 or $\frac{6}{10} = \frac{3}{5}$ are shaded.

2. **Choice B is correct.**

$\frac{12}{8} = 1.5$, the only option that is greater than 1.5 is $\frac{5}{2} \cdot \frac{5}{2} = 2.5, 2.5 > 1.5$

3. **Choice D is correct.**

If $\frac{1}{3}$ of a number is greater than 8, the number must be greater than 24. $\frac{1}{3}x > 8 \rightarrow$ multiply both sides of the inequality by 3, then: $x > 24$

4. **Choice E is correct.**

$4 \times (M + N) = 20$, then $M + N = 5$. $M > 0 \rightarrow N$ could not be 5. It must be less than 5.

5. **Choice C is correct.**

The closest to 5.03 is 5 in the choices provided.

6. **Choice C is correct.**

The ratio of lions to tigers is 10 to 6 or 5 to 3 at the zoo. Therefore, total number of lions and tigers must be divisible by 8. $5 + 3 = 8$.

From the numbers provided, only 98 is not divisible by 8.

7. **Choice C is correct.**

A represents digit 4 in the multiplication. $14 \times 342 = 4,788$

8. **Choice E is correct.**

N is even. Let's choose 2 and 4 for N. Now, let's review the options provided.

A) $\frac{N}{2} = \frac{2}{2} = 1, \frac{N}{2} = \frac{4}{2} = 2,$ One result is odd and the other one is even.

B) $N + 4 = 2 + 4 = 6, 4 + 4 = 8,$ Both results are even.

C) $2N = 2 \times 2 = 4, 4 \times 2 = 8,$ Both results are even.

www.EffortlessMath.com

D) $(2 \times N) + 2 = (2 \times 2) + 2 = 6,\ (4 \times 2) + 2 = 10,$ Both results are even.

E) $N + 1 = 2 + 1 = 3, 4 + 1 = 5,$ Both results are odd.

9.   Choice B is correct.

$8.9 - 4.08 = 4.82$, which is closest to 4.8

10.   Choice A is correct.

The value of digit 5 in both numbers x and y are in the tens place. Therefore, they have the same value.

11.   Choice C is correct.

$5 + x = 20 \rightarrow x = 15 \rightarrow 15 + 25 = 40$

12.   Choice C is correct.

$$\frac{2 + 5 + 6 \times 1 + 1}{5 + 3} = \frac{14}{8} = \frac{7}{4}$$

13.   Choice B is correct.

Area of a square $=$ *(one side)* $\times$ *(one side)* $= 2 \times 2 = 4$

14.   Choice D is correct.

$20 = x \times 4 \rightarrow x = 20 \div 4 = 5$

x equals to 5. Let's review the choices provided:

A) $x + 4 \rightarrow 5 + 4 = 9,$ 20 is not divisible by 9.
B) $2x - 4 \rightarrow 2 \times 5 - 4 = 6,$ 20 is not divisible by 6.
C) $x - 2 \rightarrow 5 - 2 = 3,$ 20 is not divisible by 3.
D) $x \times 4 \rightarrow 5 \times 4 = 20,$ 20 is divisible by 20.
E) $x + 1 \rightarrow 5 + 1 = 6,$ 20 is not divisible by 6.

Only Choice D provide the correct answer.

15.   Choice C is correct.

$x + 12 = 18 \rightarrow x = 6,$ $16 + y = 21 \rightarrow y = 5,$ $x + y = 6 + 5 = 11$

16.   Choice D is correct.

$\frac{5}{4} \times \frac{6}{2} = \frac{30}{8} = \frac{15}{4}$, Choice D is equal to $\frac{15}{4}$, $\frac{5 \times 3}{4} = \frac{15}{4}$

17.   Choice B is correct.

$5 + 3N = 41 \rightarrow 3N = 41 - 5 = 36 \rightarrow N = 12$

18. Choice D is correct.

$15 - 20 = -5$, The temperature at midnight was 5 degrees below zero.

19. Choice B is correct.

Area of a triangle $= \frac{1}{2} \times (base) \times (height) = \frac{1}{2} \times 5 \times 8 = 20$

20. Choice D is correct.

$area\ of\ a\ square = side \times side$

21. Choice A is correct.

Find the pattern: $2 + 3 = 5 \rightarrow 5 + 4 = 9 \rightarrow 9 + 5 = 14 \rightarrow 14 + 6 = 20 \rightarrow 20 + 7 = 27$

22. Choice B is correct.

$$average = \frac{sum\ of\ all\ numbers}{number\ of\ numbers} = \frac{6 + 10 + 12 + 23 + 45}{5} = 19.2$$

23. Choice B is correct.

There are 8 red ball and 20 are total number of balls. Therefore, probability that John will pick

out a red ball from the basket is 8 out of 20 or $\frac{8}{8+12} = \frac{8}{20} = \frac{2}{5}$.

24. Choice C is correct.

An equilateral triangle has 3 lines of symmetry.

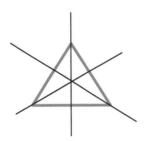

25. Choice B is correct.

10 percent of $200 = 10\%$ of $200 = \frac{10}{100} \times 200 = 20$

26. Choice C is correct.

Let's review the options provided:

A) $2 \times 2 = 4$ This is true!

B) $(4 + 1) \times 5 = 25$ This is true!

C) $6 \div (3 - 1) = 1 \rightarrow 6 \div 2 = 3$ This is NOT true!

D) $6 \times (4 - 2) = 12 \rightarrow 6 \times 2 = 12$ This is true!

E) $(10 + 23) \times 10 = 330 \rightarrow 33 \times 10 = 330$ This is true!

27. Choice D is correct.

The shape has 6 equal sides. And one side is 4. Then, the perimeter of the shape is: $4 \times 6 = 24$

28. Choice C is correct.

$$\frac{4}{5} - \frac{3}{5} = \frac{1}{5} = 0.2$$

29. Choice D is correct.

$N = 2$, then: $\frac{64}{2} + 4 = 32 + 4 = 36$

30. Choice D is correct.

Four people can paint 4 houses in 10 days. It means that for painting 8 houses in 10 days we need 8 people. To paint 8 houses in 5 days, 16 people are needed.

SSAT Lower Level Quantitative Practice Test 2

1. Choice D is correct.

$$\frac{8}{2} - \frac{3}{2} = \frac{5}{2} = 2.5$$

2. Choice B is correct.

$$48 = 3 \times N + 12 \rightarrow 3N = 48 - 12 = 36 \rightarrow N = 12$$

3. Choice A is correct.

There are 5 shaded squares. Then, the area of the shaded shades squares is: $8 \times 5 = 40 \ cm^2$

4. Choice E is correct.

$$\frac{x}{15} + 9 = 11 \rightarrow \frac{x}{15} = 11 - 9 = 2 \rightarrow \frac{x}{15} = 2 \rightarrow x = 15 \times 2 = 30$$

5. Choice C is correct.

Only choice C provides the correct equation: $3 + (4 \times N) = 23 \rightarrow 4N + 3 = 23$

6. Choice D is correct.

78 divided by 5, the remainder is 3. 45 divided by 7, the remainder is also 3.

7. Choice A is correct.

$2,400 - 606 = 1,794$

8. Choice C is correct.

All angles in a triangle sum up to 180 degrees. The triangle provided is an isosceles triangle. In an isosceles triangle, the three angles are 45, 45, and 90 degrees. Therefore, the value of x is 45.

9. Choice B is correct.

5 percent of $480 = \frac{5}{100} \times 480 = \frac{1}{20} \times 480 = \frac{480}{20} = 24$

10. Choice B is correct.

The ratio of red marbles to blue marbles is 3 to 2. Therefore, the total number of marbles must be divisible by 5. $3 + 2 = 5$. 32 is the only one that is not divisible by 5.

11. Choice D is correct.

Area of a square = side × side = 81 → side = 9, Perimeter of a square = 4 × side =
$4 \times 9 = 36$

12. Choice D is correct.

Find the pattern: $39 + 2 = 41, 41 + 3 = 44, 44 + 4 = 48, 48 + 5 = 53$

13. Choice D is correct.

The length of the rectangle is 18. Then, its width is 6. $18 \div 3 = 6$,

Perimeter of a rectangle = 2 × width + 2 × length $= 2 \times 6 + 2 \times 18 = 12 + 36 = 48$

14. Choice C is correct.

Mary's Money $= y$, John's Money $= y + 10$, John gives Mary $12 \rightarrow y + 10 - 12 = y - 2$

15. Choice E is correct.

Dividing 107 by 6 leaves a remainder of 5.

16. Choice C is correct.

$6,000 + A - 200 = 7,400 \rightarrow 6,000 + A = 7,400 + 200 = 7,600 \rightarrow$

$A = 7,600 - 6,000 = 1,600$

17. Choice E is correct.

$75 off is the same as 15 percent off. Thus, 15 percent of a number is 75. Then: 15% *of* $x =$

$75 \rightarrow 0.15x = 75 \rightarrow x = \frac{75}{0.15} = 500$.

18. Choice B is correct.

Blue marker could be found in the shaded part of this diagram because there is blue marker in
both circles.

19. Choice A is correct.

$x + 3 = 6 \rightarrow x = 3, \quad 2y = 8 \rightarrow y = 4, \qquad y - x = 4 - 3 = 1$

20. Choice C is correct.

$310 - x + 116 = 225 \rightarrow 310 - x = 225 - 116 = 109 \rightarrow x = 310 - 109 = 201$

21. Choice E is correct.

$$2\frac{1}{2} + 3\frac{1}{2} + 1\frac{1}{2} = \frac{5}{2} + \frac{7}{2} + \frac{3}{2} = \frac{15}{2} = 7\frac{1}{2}$$

22. Choice C is correct.

$$8.08 - 5.6 = 2.48$$

23. Choice D is correct.

$$500 + \square - 180 = 1{,}100 \rightarrow 500 + \square = 1{,}100 + 180 = 1{,}280 \rightarrow \square = 1{,}280 - 500 = 780.$$

24. Choice E is correct.

$\frac{1}{6}$ of students are girls. Therefore, $\frac{5}{6}$ of students in the class are boys. $\frac{5}{6}$ of 60 is 50. There are 50 boys in the class. $\frac{5}{6} \times 60 = \frac{300}{6} = 50$

25. Choice A is correct.

$$N \times (5 - 3) = 12 \rightarrow N \times 2 = 12 \rightarrow N = 6$$

26. Choice C is correct.

If $x \blacksquare y = 3x + y - 2$, Then: $4 \blacksquare 12 = 3(4) + 12 - 2 = 12 + 12 - 2 = 22$

27. Choice C is correct.

Of the numbers provided, 0.8923 is the greatest.

28. Choice A is correct.

$$\frac{7}{8} - \frac{3}{4} = \frac{7}{8} - \frac{6}{8} = \frac{1}{8} = 0.125$$

29. Choice A is correct.

The closest number to 4.02 is 4.

30. Choice E is correct.

Only choice E provides a false statement: $14 \div (2 + 5) = 14 \div 7 = 2$ is not 5

SSAT Lower Level Quantitative Practice Test 3

1. Choice A is correct.

There are 60 seconds in a minute. 60 divided by 12 is 5. She twirls her hair 5 times in a minute.

2. Choice D is correct.

Use cross multiplication to solve for the unknown:

$\frac{2}{8} = \frac{\blacksquare}{56} \rightarrow 8 \times \blacksquare = 2 \times 56 \rightarrow 8 \times \blacksquare = 112 \rightarrow \blacksquare = \frac{112}{8} = 14.$

3. Choice A is correct.

The digit 9 is in the tenth place. Then, its value is 9 tenth.

4. Choice A is correct.

$$\frac{3 \times (6+5)}{33} = \frac{3 \times 11}{33} = \frac{33}{33} = 1$$

5. Choice C is correct.

$$x + 2y - 12 = y \rightarrow x + y - 12 = 0, \text{then: } x + y = 12$$

6. Choice D is correct.

First, find the pattern. In the first row, the sum of two numbers 1 and 3 are provided. So $1 + 3 = 2^2$. In the second row, there are three numbers 1, 3 and 5. Then: $1 + 3 + 5 = 3^2$.

In the question statement, there are nine numbers. Then, the answer is 9^2.

7. Choice A is correct.

B represents digit 2 in the multiplication. $15 \times 425 = 6,375$.

8. Choice E is correct.

N is odd. Let's choose 1 and 3 for N. Now, Let's review the choices provided.

A) $(2 \times N) + 1 = (2 \times 1) + 1 = 3, (2 \times 3) + 1 = 7,$ Both results are odd.

B) $N + 2 = 1 + 2 = 3, 3 + 2 = 5,$ Both results are odd.

C) $3N = 1 \times 3 = 3, 3 \times 3 = 9,$ Both results are odd.

D) $(3 \times N) + 2 = (3 \times 1) + 2 = 5, (3 \times 3) + 2 = 11,$ Both results are odd.

E) $2N = 2 \times 1 = 2, 2 \times 3 = 6,$ Both results are even.

Choice E is always an even number.

9. Choice B is correct.

$9.5 - 5.08 = 4.42$, which is closest to 4.4

10. Choice C is correct.

There are 4 shaded triangles and 5 unshaded triangles. There are 9 triangles and 4 of them are shaded. Then, $\frac{4}{9}$ of the shape is shaded.

11. Choice B is correct.

From the choices provided, choice B gives a better estimate: $2.15 \approx 2$ and $186 \approx 200$.

$2.15 \times 186 \approx 2 \times 200$

12. Choice A is correct.

The shaded region shows people who drink hot chocolate and green tea.

13. Choice E is correct.

Area of the rectangle is: $length \times width = 4 \times 3 = 12$

14. Choice B is correct.

Only Choice (B) shows a line of symmetry.

15. Choice A is correct.

$x + 3 = 9 \rightarrow x = 9 - 3 = 6$

$19 + y = 25 \rightarrow y = 25 - 19 = 6$

$x - y = 6 - 6 = 0$

16. Choice D is correct.

$\frac{2}{5} \times \frac{10}{4} = \frac{20}{20} = 1$, Choice D is equal to: $\frac{5 \times 4}{20} = \frac{20}{20} = 1$

17. Choice B is correct.

$8 + 5 \times A = 83 \rightarrow 5 \times A = 83 - 8 = 75 \rightarrow A = 15$

18. Choice D is correct.

3 pages in 42 minutes means Mike read one page in 14 minutes. If he wants to read 25 pages, that it will take $25 \times 14 = 350$ minutes.

19. Choice B is correct.

Point A shows 4.4 on the diagram, then $A - 2.3 = 4.4 - 2.3 = 2.1$

20. Choice B is correct.

$$area\ of\ a\ triangle = \frac{1}{2} \times (base) \times (height)$$

21. Choice A is correct.

Find the pattern: $3 + 3 = 6 \to 6 + 4 = 10 \to 10 + 5 = 15 \to 15 + 6 = 21 \to 21 + 7 = 28$

22. Choice B is correct.

Shape A is a tetrahedron, B is a cone, C is a pyramid, D is a triangular prism and E is a cylinder.

So, choice B is correct.

23. Choice B is correct.

According to the graph, the slice labeled "bus" represents about $\frac{1}{4}$ of the entire pie. Since a total

of 400 vehicle were sold, $\frac{1}{4} \times 400 = 100$ buses were sold.

24. Choice D is correct.

The perimeter of a square is $60\ cm$. Then, one side of the square is $15\ cm$: $60 \div 4 = 15$

Area of a square = one side × one side $= 15 \times 15 = 225$

25. Choice B is correct.

10 percent of $300 = 10\%$ of $300 = \frac{10}{100} \times 300 = 30$

26. Choice C is correct.

Let's review the choices provided:

A) $3 \times (5 - 2) = 9$,   This is true!

B) $(3 + 2) \times 5 = 25$,   This is true!

C) $6 \div (4 - 1) = 1 \to 6 \div 3 = 1$,   This is NOT true!

D) $6 \times (4 - 2) = 12 \to 6 \times 2 = 12$,   This is true!

E) $(8 + 25) \times 10 = 330 \to 33 \times 10 = 330$,   This is true!

27. Choice E is correct.

Perimeter of a polygon = number of sides × side $\to 72 = 8 \times side \to side = \frac{72}{8} = 9$

28. Choice C is correct.

$\frac{4}{5} - \frac{2}{5} = \frac{2}{5} = 0.4$

29. Choice B is correct.

$C = 8$, then: $19 - (56 \div C) - 8 = \square \rightarrow 19 - (56 \div 8) - 8 = 19 - 7 - 8 = 4$

30. Choice C is correct.

Tom and Oliver are driving at the same speed. $32 \div 16 = 2$, their speed is 2 *miles per minute*.

Then: 52 *miles* $\times \frac{1 \ minute}{2 \ miles} = 26$ *minutes*

SSAT Lower Level Quantitative Practice Test 4

1.   Choice E is correct.

$$\frac{8}{2} - \frac{5}{2} = \frac{3}{2} = 1.5$$

2.   Choice B is correct.

$$48 = 2 \times A + 10 \rightarrow 2 \times A = 48 - 10 = 38 \rightarrow A = 19$$

3.   Choice A is correct.

When folded, the shape will become a cylinder. A cylinder can be made up of a rectangle and two circles.

4.   Choice D is correct.

Whole numbers Between 3 and 7 is {4,5,6} also between 5 and 8 is {6,7}. Then: $P = 6$

5.   Choice C is correct.

When you solve, choice (C) becomes $31 = 33$, which is the only false statement.

6.   Choice D is correct.

4 miles in half an hour $4 \times 2 = 8$ miles per hour.

7.   Choice A is correct.

The decimal 0.709 is equivalent to $\frac{709}{1,000}$, which is the biggest number given. The farther away a digit is to the right of the decimal point, the smaller the place that digit is in.

8.   Choice C is correct.

The number of items in the cart must be a multiple of 2. From the choices provided, only 28 is divisible by 2.

9.   Choice A is correct.

There are 2 shaded triangles and 4 unshaded triangles There are 6 triangles and 2 of them are shaded. Then, the shaded part is: $\frac{2}{6} = \frac{1}{3}$.

10. Choice A is correct.

More of the circle is shaded, so the number has to be smaller than 350. Only choice A is less than 350.

11. Choice B is correct.

$900 - 700 = 200$

12. Choice D is correct.

2 thousandth is the correct awnser.

13. Choice D is correct.

The diameter is the full length across the circle. The radius is the length halfway across the circle. If we're given that the diameter is $18\ cm$, the radius is half of that: $18 \div 2 = 9\ cm$.

14. Choice C is correct.

$\$50 - \$27.45 = \$22.55$. You must line up the decimal points and subtract.

15. Choice B is correct.

Dividing 150 by 4 leaves a remainder of 2. $150 \div 4 = 37\ r2$

16. Choice C is correct.

$5,000 + A - 200 = 7,400 \rightarrow 5,000 + A = 7,400 + 200 = 7,600 \rightarrow$
$A = 7,600 - 5,000 = 2,600$

17. Choice D is correct.

16 percent of $250 = 16\%$ of $250 = \frac{16}{100} \times 250 = 40$

18. Choice A is correct.

Only choice A is less than $\frac{5}{2}$: $\frac{5}{2} = 2.5 > 1.07$

19. Choice A is correct.

$\frac{x}{2} - 2 = 6 \rightarrow \frac{x}{2} = 6 + 2 \rightarrow \frac{x}{2} = 8 \rightarrow x = 2 \times 8 \rightarrow x = 16$

$2y + 4 = 20 \rightarrow 2y = 20 - 4 \rightarrow 2y = 16$

$x - 2y = 16 - 16 = 0$

20. Choice C is correct.

$125 - y + 16 = 17 \rightarrow y = 125 + 16 - 17 \rightarrow y = 124$

21. Choice C is correct.

25 percent of $54.00 is $13.5. (Remember that 25 percent is equal to one fourth)

22. Choice A is correct.

$\dfrac{9}{20} - \dfrac{7}{20} = \dfrac{9-7}{20} = \dfrac{2}{20} = \dfrac{1}{10} = 0.1$

23. Choice A is correct.

$1,200 - \square + \dfrac{1,800}{2} = 400 + 700 \rightarrow 1,200 - \square + 900 = 1,100 \rightarrow$

$\square = 1200 + 900 - 1,100 = 1,000$

24. Choice E is correct.

$12 \times \dfrac{3}{4} = 9$ hours

25. Choice A is correct.

$N \times (5 - 2) = 12 \rightarrow N \times 3 = 12 \rightarrow N = 4$

26. Choice D is correct.

If $a \blacklozenge b = 2a - b$, Then: $1 \blacklozenge 4 = 2a - b = 2 \times 1 - 4 = 2 - 4 = -2$

27. Choice C is correct.

Of the numbers provided, 0.9923 is the greatest.

28. Choice E is correct.

$\dfrac{7}{10} + \dfrac{1}{2} = \dfrac{7+5}{10} = \dfrac{12}{10} = \dfrac{6}{5} = 1.2$

29. Choice A is correct.

The closest number to 125.06 is 125.

30. Choice B is correct.

$(2 \times 5 + 4) = (7 + 3 \times 2) \rightarrow 14 = 13$, Choice B is not correct.

SSAT Lower Level Quantitative Practice Test 5

1. **Choice E is correct.**

$$\frac{8}{3} - \frac{4}{3} = \frac{4}{3} = 1\frac{1}{3}$$

2. **Choice B is correct.**

$$58 = 3 \times \Delta + 10 \rightarrow 3 \times \Delta = 58 - 10 = 48 \rightarrow \Delta = \frac{48}{3} = 16$$

3. **Choice A is correct.**

$$a = b + 2c, b = c \rightarrow a = c + 2c = 3c$$

4. **Choice B is correct.**

$$8 = y - 12 \rightarrow y = 8 + 12 = 20$$

5. **Choice E is correct.**

$550 - 200P =?$ →The answer cannot be determined from the information given. We cannot add numbers with unknown variables.

6. **Choice D is correct.**

(A) (A) $30 \times \frac{2}{3} = 20$ It is a whole number.

(B) $3 + 9 = 12$ It is a whole number.

(C) $\frac{104}{4} = 26$ It is a whole number.

(D) $\frac{1}{6} \times 9 = \frac{9}{6} = 1.5$ It is NOT a whole number.

(E) $19.5 + 3.5 = 23$ It is a whole number.

7. **Choice C is correct.**

Since this is a race time, for Maria to beat the record means her time is a twentieth of a *second* or 0.05 *second* less than the record. To find the answer, subtract 0.05 from 17.21. Then:

$$17.21 - 0.05 = 17.16$$

8. **Choice C is correct.**

The shape has been reflected. (flipped as if in a mirror).

9.   Choice B is correct.

$$\frac{5}{100} \times 360 = \frac{5 \times 360}{100} = 18$$

10.   Choice C is correct.

$$2,880 \div 60 = 48$$

11.   Choice B is correct.

The three angles on the line add up to 180 degrees. Then:

$$180 = 25 + 30 + \alpha \rightarrow 180 - 55 = \alpha \rightarrow \alpha = 125$$

12.   Choice D is correct.

The number on the right-hand column skip by four: $10, 14, 18, 22$ (and are $14 - 1.5 = 12.5$ more than the number in the left column). 22 plus 4 is 26 (and 13.5 plus 12.5 is 26). So that must be the missing number.

13.   Choice D is correct.

4 cubed is $4 \times 4 \times 4 = 64$

14.   Choice C is correct.

James's age: $7 \times 5 = 35$.

15.   Choice B is correct.

The place value of 8 in 962.581 is hundredths. Then, the value of 8 is 8 hundredths.

16.   Choice D is correct.

$$2500 = 600 + C - 1900 \rightarrow 2,500 + 1900 - 600 = C \rightarrow C = 3800$$

17.   Choice C is correct.

The correct answer is square pyramid.

18.   Choice A is correct.

Only choice A is less than $\frac{7}{2}$: $\frac{7}{2} = 3.5 > 2.4$

19.   Choice B is correct.

$$x - 8 = 7 \rightarrow x = 7 + 8 = 15, y - 7 = 9 \rightarrow y = 9 + 7 = 16$$

$$2 \times y - 2 \times x = 2(16) - 2(15) = 32 - 30 = 2$$

20. Choice C is correct.

$$250 - 2y + 30 = 230 \rightarrow 2y = 280 - 230 \rightarrow y = \frac{50}{2} = 25$$

21. Choice A is correct.

$$50 + n = 50 \rightarrow n = 50 - 50 = 0, 50 \times n = 50 \times 0 = 0$$

22. Choice C is correct.

$$12.58 + 5.5 - 2.85 = 15.23$$

23. Choice C is correct.

$$\square - \left(\frac{500}{2}\right) + (2 \times 300) = \left(\frac{1,800}{2}\right) \rightarrow \square = 900 + 250 - 600 = 550$$

24. Choice E is correct.

The coordinate of the point D is: $(6, -1)$

25. Choice C is correct.

There are 18 triangles in the figure and 9 of them are shaded. Then, the shaded part of the figure is: $\frac{9}{18} = \frac{9 \div 9}{18 \div 9} = \frac{1}{2}$

26. Choice C is correct.

Only choice C equals to 128.89.

$$128.89 = 128 + 0.89 = 128 + \frac{89}{100} = 128 + \frac{8}{10} + \frac{9}{100} = 128 + \frac{8}{10} + \frac{6}{100} + \frac{3}{100}$$

27. Choice C is correct.

The greatest number is 0.7923.

28. Choice B is correct.

$$\frac{20}{8} - \frac{1}{2} - \frac{2}{4} = \frac{5}{2} - \frac{1}{2} - \frac{1}{2} = \frac{3}{2} = 1.5$$

29. Choice A is correct.

The closest number to 7.06 is 7.

30. Choice E is correct.

Only choice (E) is a false statement: $\left(\frac{8}{2} \times \frac{5}{2}\right) = (4 \times 5) \rightarrow 10 = 20$

"Effortless Math" Publications

Effortless Math authors' team strives to prepare and publish the best quality Mathematics learning resources to make learning Math easier for all. We hope that our publications help you or your student Math in an effective way.

We all in Effortless Math wish you good luck and successful studies!

Effortless Math Authors

www.EffortlessMath.com

... So Much More Online!

✓ FREE Math lessons

✓ More Math learning books!

✓ Mathematics Worksheets

✓ Online Math Tutors

Need a PDF version of this book?

Please visit www.EffortlessMath.com

Receive the PDF version of this book or get another FREE book!

Thank you for using our Book!

Do you LOVE this book?

Then, you can get the PDF version of this book or another book absolutely FREE!

Please email us at:

info@EffortlessMath.com

for details.

Made in United States
Troutdale, OR
02/28/2024

18008566R00053